MW00379557

This book belongs to:

____

Made in the USA
Monee, IL
08 December 2022

20359571R00069